D1298002

How to Build a DINOSAUR

Written by Elena Martin

Harcourt Achieve
Rigby • Saxon • Steck-Vaughn

www.HarcourtAchieve.com
1.800.531.5015

Contents

You might have seen **dinosaur** bones before. And you know that dinosaurs lived a very long time ago—but have you ever wondered how a dinosaur is built?

It's a **paleontologist's** job to find the dinosaur bones and get them ready for people to see. Here are the steps they use to build a dinosaur!

DIG IT UP

Dinosaur bones are found in the ground. When a new dinosaur **skeleton** is found, it needs to be dug up. Paleontologists have to dig very carefully so the bones don't break.

First, they draw a line around the bones. Special tools are used to break up the rock around them. Then more rock is chipped away. Soon, only the bones are left!

WRAP IT UP

Next, the bones are wrapped up. This keeps them safe when they are moved.

Cloth and **plaster** are wrapped around the bones to make a special jacket. This is the same way the doctor makes a cast if you break your arm! Like a cast, the jacket protects what is inside of it.

5

LABEL IT

Then, the dinosaur bones are **labeled**. Paleontologists write down what each bone is. Each one gets its own special number.

Labeling helps keep the dinosaur bones from getting lost or mixed up. And it makes it easier to put the bones back together at the **museum**.

MOVE IT

Next, the dinosaur bones are moved to the museum where they will be **displayed**.

Dinosaur bones wrapped in plaster are very heavy. Some bones are so heavy that a **helicopter** is needed to lift them. Trucks are used to carry smaller bones to the museum.

GET IT READY

Soon, the bones are at the museum. It's time to get them ready to be displayed. The bones are taken out of their jackets and cleaned. Broken bones are fixed.

Sometimes the bones are copied. The museum displays the copies instead of the real bones. This keeps the real bones safe.

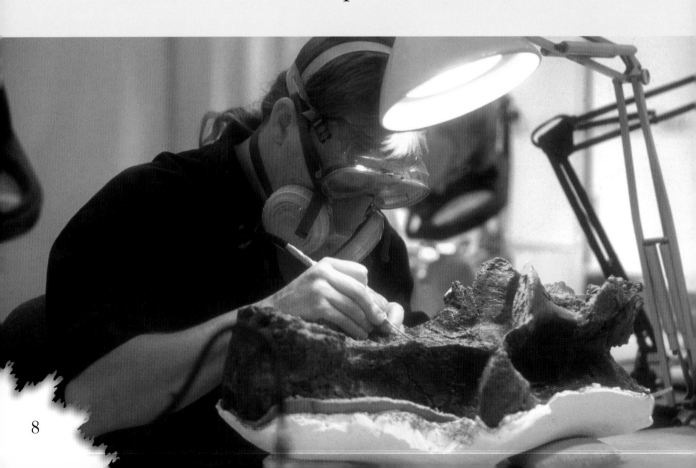

MAKE A BLUEPRINT

Next, paleontologists make a **blueprint**, a special kind of map. It shows how the bones go together.

To make the blueprint, paleontologists use what they know about dinosaurs. They plan where to put the bones so they will look just right.

9

Put It Together

The blueprint is done. All that's left is to put the bones together! That might sound easy. But workers have to make sure each bone goes in exactly the right place. It must be held so it won't come loose.

It takes paleontologists many months to put together a dinosaur skeleton!

SHOW IT OFF

Finally, the dinosaur is ready. It is time to show it off in an **exhibit**! Everyone who comes to the museum can see it.

Adults and children come from all over to see a new exhibit. They learn about the dinosaur. One day, some of those children might even build their own dinosaurs!

11

GLOSSARY

blueprint   a special map for building something

dinosaur   a kind of animal that lived a very long time ago

displayed   showed to everyone

exhibit   something that is shown to everyone

helicopter   a flying machine that can carry very heavy things

labeled   marked with a name or number

museum   a building where people can go to see special things from art and science

paleontologist   a person who studies dinosaurs

plaster   a paste that gets hard when it dries

skeleton   the part of an animal that is made of bone

Justin's Big Fish

Written by Debra Lucas
Illustrated by Kathryn Mitter

Harcourt Achieve

Rigby · Saxon · Steck-Vaughn

www.HarcourtAchieve.com
1.800.531.5015

Contents

Lucky Lewis

Justin sat down on the couch, ready to watch his favorite show. Suddenly, the front door opened, and his friend Lewis ran in.

"Look at this!" he shouted. Lewis always rang the doorbell. But this time he just ran in the house.

"You scared me!" said Justin. "What's going on?"

"Look who's on the front page of the newspaper!" Lewis said. Lewis handed the newspaper to Justin.

"That's me!" said Lewis.

Sure enough, there was a picture of Lewis on the front page. He was holding up a huge fish and grinning. The headline read, "Big Fish Is Rare Catch."

"My dad took me to the river over the weekend," Lewis said. "I was half asleep when WHAM, I caught this huge fish! My dad took that picture of me. People keep coming up to me on the street. They say they've never seen a fish so big!"

Justin was happy for Lewis. But he wished that he could catch a big fish, too.

The Surprise Trip

The next day Justin's dad had a surprise for him. "We're going on a hiking trip!" he said. "Everything is packed."

"But I want to go fishing, not hiking," Justin said.

"Come on, Justin," said his dad. "It will be fun! We'll get out in the fresh air and see some animals. . . ."

"The only animal I want to see is a big fish, like the one Lewis caught!" said Justin.

"I'm happy for Lewis," his dad said, "but everything is already planned for the hiking trip. It's too late to change it now."

A Big Find

It was a perfect day for a hike. The sun was warm, and a breeze was blowing. Justin tried to have fun. He liked being with his dad. But he just couldn't help feeling jealous of Lewis.

"One day," Justin thought, "I'll catch a big fish. Then I can get my picture in the paper, too."

After they hiked for a while, Justin and his dad stopped to rest. Justin noticed a strange rock in the dirt. He dug it up.

"Hey!" Justin said. "I think there's something in this rock."

"Let's see," said his dad. Justin held the rock carefully. His dad poured water on it to wash the dirt off. And there it was—the fossil of a fish!

In the News

When they got home, Justin and his dad looked through Justin's big book on fossils.

"I think this is it!" Justin said. He pointed to the fins and sharp teeth.

"It sure is," said his dad. "This fish lived millions of years ago. The book says not many people find a fossil this big."

"I have to go tell Lewis about *my* fish!" said Justin.

The next time Lewis came to Justin's house, Justin had something to show him.

"Lewis, look at what's in the newspaper today!" Justin said. He held up the paper for Lewis to see. On the front page was a picture of Justin with his fish fossil. The headline read in big letters, "Big Fossil Is Rare Find."

"Now I have a big fish, too!" Justin said.

Big Fossil
Is Rare Find

Close AND Turn

INDEX

Close AND Turn